The Sound of the Spirit

of the

at Spirit Baptism

John David Clark, Sr.

The Sound of the Spirit at Spirit Baptism
© 2008   John David Clark, Sr.

ISBN-13: 978–1-934782-01-9

First printing, 1980 (as chapter five of the book, *Pentecostal Light*)
Second printing, 1991 (as chapter five of the book, *Spiritual Light*)
Third printing, 2008 (under the title, *Speaking in Tongues at Spirit Baptism*)
Fourth printing, 2023

----

cover design and graphics by Donna Nelson

For information, write to:

Books – The Sound of the Spirit
PO Box 99
Burlington, NC 27216-0099

For more information, please visit these helpful websites:
www.PastorJohnsHouse.com
www.GoingtoJesus.com
www.Isaiah58.com
www.youtube.com/TheSpiritIstheWitness

And for good music all day long, go to:
www.SongsofRest.com

Author's Notes

- In English, the singular and plural forms of "you" are identical. However, in biblical Hebrew and Greek, there are obvious differences. Therefore, to more perfectly convey the biblical writers' messages in verses where the English word "you" appears, I have italicized the "y" of all plural forms, such as *y*ou, *y*our, *y*ours, and *y*ourselves.

- Translations of Old and New Testament scriptures are my own. Following standard practice, whenever a word is added to the translation for clarification, that word is italicized.

- Unless otherwise noted, the Greek text used is the Byzantine text as found in *THE NEW TESTAMENT IN THE ORIGINAL GREEK*, compiled and arranged by Maurice A. Robinson and William G. Pierpont, Chilton Book Publishing, 2005.

- Conflicting rules exist as to how punctuation should be used, none of them being adequate for every situation. My Readers will find that I subscribe to a freer punctuation style. Of special note, I do not include within quotation marks any punctuation that is not a part of what is quoted. To do otherwise, in my opinion, leaves too much room for misrepresentation of the original author's intent.

Introduction

Any place, any time, and in a variety of circumstances, people may receive the experience which Jesus described to Nicodemus as being "born again" (Jn. 3:3). Jesus also told that Jewish elder that a definite sign would accompany each new birth: a sound produced by the Spirit. He said, "The wind blows wherever it will, and you hear its sound. . . . So is everyone who is born of the Spirit" (Jn. 3:8).

In Acts, when men began receiving the Spirit, the stories of new birth which mention the sound of the Spirit tell us that the sound was speaking in tongues (Acts 2, 10, 19), and it may even be a heavenly language of angels, unknown on earth (1Cor. 13:1). So, it may or may not be a language understood by those standing by. A young woman received the Spirit in my home one morning as we were praying, and she began to make a clicking sound. At first, I did not know where the sound was coming from, or even that a human was making it. But I soon realized that it was coming from her. A few weeks later, while watching a documentary on television, I heard the same clicking sound and was amazed to learn that it was part of the language of a tribe in the middle of Africa!

For another example, a well-known evangelist told of being troubled by the unusual sound that a woman began making in his meeting while praying for the baptism of the Spirit. The next day at lunch, he said, while telling those in his party about it, he was approached by a woman who was sitting at the next table and had overheard him. She introduced herself as a missionary who had spent decades in China. Then she said that she had been there the previous evening and had heard the unusual sounds which the praying woman had made. It was a language from a remote part of China where she herself had done mission work, she told the evangelist, and she even had understood what the woman who received the Spirit was saying.

Jesus did not tell Nicodemus that the sound which the Spirit makes when someone is born again would always make us comfortable; he just said we would always hear it. Nor did Jesus tell Nicodemus that the sound of the Spirit would always be a discernible language. Paul even suggested that the sound of the Spirit may even be a kind of groaning. "The Spirit itself intercedes for us", he said, "with groanings beyond words" (Rom. 8:26). As one brother wisely said, "God can be right any kinda way He wants to!" And that means the Spirit can make any kinda sound God wants it to.

It is remarkable that in videos from around the globe, the sound of believers speaking in tongues and worshipping God seems familiar. It is not that the languages themselves are familiar, to be sure, but the sound communicates a familiar feeling to those who also have received the Spirit.

That sweet sound of the Spirit (specifically, speaking in tongues) is not mentioned every time the New Testament tells of people being born again, but we cannot be wrong to assume that it was heard in each case because Jesus said it would be. This book will consider in some depth that holy sound, the sign which Jesus said would accompany every new birth experience, and show why men need that sign to be given.

The Sound of the Spirit

of the Spirit

at Spirit Baptism

John David Clark, Sr.

Blessed are the people who know the joyful shout;
they shall walk, O Lord, in the light of your countenance!
Psalm 89:15

THE BAPTISM OF THE SPIRIT IS THE NEW BIRTH

It is an understatement to say that confusion and controversy exist among Christians concerning the baptism of the holy Spirit. Traditionally, Pentecostal Christians have taught that one is born again before receiving the baptism of the holy Ghost and that when a person receives that baptism, he will speak in tongues. Non-Pentecostal Christians, on the other hand, teach that to be born again means that one has received the baptism of the Spirit, but they deny that a sound from the Spirit always accompanies it. They disregard, with various degrees of confidence, the testimonies of the Pentecostal community about speaking in tongues when one is baptized with the Spirit. In spite of the differences, however, there is truth in both camps.

In the New Testament, the new birth experience is described in various ways, such as "conversion", "sanctification", "redemption", being "born of the Spirit", etc. And contrary to the traditional Pentecostal stance, the new birth is also referred to as the baptism of the Spirit. Paul consistently taught that we are baptized by the Spirit into Christ (Rom. 6:3; 1Cor. 12:13; Gal. 3:27), and in Christ, we become a "new creature" (2Cor. 5:17; Gal. 6:15), a "new man, who in God's likeness is created in true righteousness and holiness" (Eph. 4:24) and walks "in newness of life" (Rom. 6:4b). Beyond all question, to enter into Christ is to be born again, and in Christ, we find grace and salvation (2Tim. 2:1, 10), righteousness, sanctification, and redemption (1Cor. 1:30), and are given the promise of eternal life (2Tim. 1:1). Everything we need in order to obtain eternal life is there, in him, which is why Paul told the saints that "*you* are complete in him" (Col. 2:10). The traditional Pentecostal position, that the new birth is a separate experience from the baptism of the Spirit, just does not hold up to careful scrutiny. That the baptism of the Spirit is the new birth is clearly true.

"Initial Evidence"

Until fairly recently, Pentecostal denominations unshakably held that speaking in tongues is the "initial evidence" of the baptism of the holy Ghost. Historically, that doctrine is what set Pentecostal groups apart from other Christian sects, but in recent decades, among Pentecostals, there has been some movement away from that position. Many who are called "Charismatics" (the modern version of Pentecostals) disagree with the old-line Pentecostal position. Instead, they teach that while the Spirit may move one to make a divine utterance when one is baptized with it, that need not occur in every case in order for the baptism to be of God.

Pentecostals have often failed in their attempt to persuade others of their point of view because they rely so heavily on the new birth experiences recorded in the book of Acts. Using the book of Acts alone, it is impossible to determine whether or not the baptism of the holy Ghost always includes the Spirit speaking. In some accounts (Acts 2, 10, 19), the sound is mentioned, while in others (Acts 8, 9, 16), it is not. Pointing to those dissimilar accounts, opponents of the traditional Pentecostal doctrine have had justifiable criticism of the teaching that speaking in tongues is the "initial evidence" of being baptized with the Spirit.

None of this means that the millions of testimonies from Pentecostals of receiving the baptism of the Spirit and speaking in tongues is false. The Scriptures bear ample witness to people being baptized with the Spirit, with speaking in tongues being the sign that it has happened. So, how are we to proceed? If non-Pentecostals are correct in teaching that the new birth is the baptism of the Spirit, and if Pentecostals are correct in teaching that everyone who is baptized with the Spirit speaks "as the Spirit moves them to speak" (cf. Acts 2:4), then the logical conclusion is that only those who have been baptized by the Spirit and moved to make a divine utterance are born again! But is that true? Does the Bible teach that the sound of the Spirit is present *every time* someone is baptized by the Spirit into the body of Christ?

I am persuaded that the traditional Pentecostal stance in this matter is close to the truth. The only clarification I would make is that not everyone speaks in a definite language when they are baptized with the Spirit, and Jesus only said that the Spirit would make a sound through them. Therefore, I do not think that requiring the Spirit's sound lays out a path which God must follow; rather, I think it recognizes the path that God has laid out and which we must follow.

"You Can Have It."

After the outpouring of the Spirit in the Azusa Street revival of 1906, the Pentecostal experience became a matter of some controversy among believers. My father, who, as a Free Will Baptist minister, received that experience in early 1925, said that some communities in North Carolina tried to ban Pentecostal meetings in their town. He gave as an example an event that transpired in Durham, North Carolina, when officials called for a public meeting to discuss the matter, inviting Pentecostals and non-Pentecostals alike to participate. Some Pentecostal brothers asked my father to come to the meeting and represent them, and even though he did not agree altogether with the standard Pentecostal doctrine, he decided to accept the invitation.

The appointed day came, and my father was taken to an auditorium, which he found packed with people from all denominations. City officials were on the stage onto which my father and other ministers were led. All the non-Pentecostal Christians (Baptists, Methodists, Lutherans, etc.) sat on one side of the auditorium, and the Pentecostal Christians (Church of God, Pentecostal Holiness, Assembly of God, etc.) sat on the other side. The officials opened the meeting, and a few ministers spoke. Then, my father was given the opportunity to speak.

He arose and took his place before the assembly and, after some introductory remarks, said, "May I ask how many people in this auditorium today know that if a person has not received, or been 'baptized with', the holy Spirit of God, then he is not born again and does not belong to God? Let me see your hands if you believe that a person must have the holy Ghost to be born again."

All the non-Pentecostals raised their hands, but not a single Pentecostal hand went up.

"Thank you," he said. "You may put your hands down."

Then he proceeded. "Now let me ask everyone here another question. How many people here today know that when a person receives the Spirit of God, what the Bible calls the baptism of the holy Ghost, that person begins to speak in other tongues?"

At that, all the Pentecostals raised their hands, but none of the non-Pentecostals did.

"Thank you. You may put your hands down." Then, turning to face the community leaders who had called this meeting, he challenged them with one of the most brilliant insights into the confusion of Christianity that has ever been given by God to man.

"Well, I hope that now you gentlemen see the mess you have here in Durham. Over there [pointing toward the non-Pentecostals], people without the holy Ghost saying everybody must have it. And over here [pointing to the Pentecostals], you have people with the holy Ghost saying nobody needs it. If this confusion is what you want in your city, you can have it."

Needless to say, the whole assembly went into an uproar; he had made both camps angry. One outraged Christian jumped up from his seat in the auditorium and ran onto the stage where my father stood. He rubbed his curled-up fist hard against my father's face and threatened him, saying, "If what you're saying is true, my mother's in hell right now." I don't know what he expected my father to do about that, but somehow my father was able to escape him and the meeting, and return home. But the point my father made was a perceptive one, and every believer would benefit by considering it.

Our focus in this book will be to examine the Scriptures to demonstrate the wisdom in what my father told that divided assembly in Durham. And although the book of Acts contains material relevant to the issue, we must go beyond the personal experiences recorded there to mine the gold that is available throughout the Bible. This is a doctrinal issue which is as fundamentally important to the faith as can be. We must, therefore, approach the matter from a teaching perspective, drawing from the Master's words and the teachings of the apostles and prophets.

THE STATE OF MAN

There is a basic truth concerning mankind's spiritual condition that must be realized in order to perceive God's wisdom in ordaining a consistent, recognizable sign of Spirit baptism. This biblical revelation is that all mankind is, by nature, estranged from the Creator and lives in deep spiritual darkness. The ancient prophet Jeremiah described the condition of the human heart this way: "The heart is more deceitful than anything, and incurable! Who knows it?" (Jer. 17:9). The answer is that no one can know it unless God reveals it to him. We all are, or we were before Jesus rescued us, a part of this desperately wicked and deceived world. Nobody on earth is excluded from the apostle John's observation that "the whole world lies in wickedness" (1Jn. 5:19b).

Most people do not know this is true. They do not understand that their lives need changing, that there is a holy life for them to live that is different from, and contrary to, the way they are living now. This is difficult for man to believe because he can so easily deceive himself. Being in the combined darkness of ignorance and pride, he can convince himself that he is right – and then refuse to look at any contradictory evidence. When a man does not know that his own heart is "deceitful" and "incurably wicked", he has the tendency to trust his own judgment concerning himself.

The Scriptures are replete with stories of people who were convinced they were holy when they were evil. There were, and no doubt still are, many deluded souls who consider themselves to be servants of God, yet are not (cf. 2Cor. 11:13–15; 1Jn. 2:18–19; 4:1–5; Rev. 2:9; 3:9). When Paul wrote of men who considered themselves to be something in the kingdom of God that they were not (pastor, prophet, or whatever), he described them as spreading such deception to others (2Tim. 3:13). Jesus rebuked some ministers of his time with these words: "*You* are they who justify *yourselves* before men; but God knows *your* hearts" (Lk. 16:15a). And he warned his followers of a time coming when such men "will put *you* out of the synagogues. In fact, the hour is coming when anyone who kills *you* will think he's offering a service to God" (Jn. 16:2).

This, then, is the state of man. He does not know the truth, does not understand eternal life, cannot discern between good and evil, and does not appreciate the doctrines and deeds of the Spirit. And, most significantly, he does not know that he does not know. He is bound by his own darkened intellect, self-esteem, lust, and a wily, perverse heart. His spirit is restless, his work is temporal, his institutions are vain, and his desires, animalistic. As David said, "Every man in his best state is altogether vanity" (Ps. 39:5).

Man's Confession of Faith

If man, by nature, is in this miserable spiritual state, how can any human "confession of faith" be trusted? Whenever people make a confession of faith, then, it means nothing, or means nothing more than that they are making that claim. Nothing that men say makes anything true. Whether faith actually abides within a man's heart is not proved by what he says. Whatever anyone declares about himself or God can only be as dependable as his spiritual condition, and man's spiritual condition is depraved. "In me," wrote Paul, "that is, in my flesh, dwells nothing good" (Rom. 7:18). But it was not only Paul who was in this lowly condition. The whole world is wicked, just as John said. Paul even observed that the spirit in humans is so darkened that holy things seem foolish to them: "A natural man does not receive the things of the Spirit of God, for they are foolishness to him, and he cannot comprehend them because they are spiritually discerned" (1Cor. 2:14).

Jesus refused to trust the testimony of men without the Spirit: "While he was in Jerusalem at the Passover, during the feast, many believed in his name, seeing his miracles that he performed. But as for Jesus, he did not trust himself to them because he knows all men and because he had no need for anyone to testify about man, for he knew what was in man" (Jn. 2:23–25). He did not even trust the testimony of his disciples before they received it: "His disciples said to him, 'We know now that you know everything, and you have no need for anyone to question you; by this, we believe that you came from God.' Jesus answered them, 'Do *you* now believe? Behold, an hour is coming, and now has come, for *you* to be scattered, each to his own house, and to leave me alone'" (Jn. 16:29–32; cf. 6:68–70). Jesus understood man's deplorable natural state as no one else ever did. On one occasion, he bluntly stated to his listeners, "I accept the testimony of no man" (Jn. 5:34), and there is no indication that Jesus' attitude toward man's testimony has ever changed.

Scriptures such as those above reveal the worthlessness of man's estimation of his own standing with God. They show why man needs concrete, trustworthy evidence directly from God that will let him know that his confession of faith in Jesus and his repentance have been accepted and that he is forgiven. This is a chief reason for God Himself to give us a sign when He baptizes someone with His Spirit, declaring that person to be His child. It is the Spirit's testimony that counts, not merely a human one. Jesus declared plainly that the witness of the Spirit precedes one's personal confession, and makes it valid: "When the Comforter comes, whom I will send to *you* from the Father, the

Spirit of truth which comes out from the Father, he will testify of me, and *you* also will bear witness because *you*'ve been with me from the beginning" (Jn. 15:26–27).

Because man, on his own, cannot know the truth about himself or God, we must conclude that until the Spirit declares one to be born of God, there is no scriptural basis for that person to consider himself to be born again. "The Spirit is the witness", wrote John, "because the Spirit is truth" (1Jn. 5:6b). And that is the truth behind Paul's statement, "The Spirit itself bears witness, together with our spirit, that we are the children of God" (Rom. 8:16). Were it man's place to declare that he has received the Spirit (as many are taught to do), we would be in a position (as many are) of not knowing who to believe and, so, not knowing who is a brother in Christ and who is not. But if in every case, "the Spirit itself bears witness, together with our spirit, that we are the children of God," then we may discern with certainty who is born again and who is not – without making our own judgment about anyone.

The Spirit's voice being heard when a person is baptized with the Spirit is God's personal testimony to His Son, and to that person's faith in His Son. John admonished his readers never to reject God's testimony: "If we receive the witness of men, the witness of God is greater, for this is the witness of God that He has given concerning His Son. He who does not believe God has made Him a liar because he has not believed in the witness that God has given concerning His Son" (1Jn. 5:9, 10b). Likewise, the author of Hebrews gave us this arresting admonition: "Beware that *you* do not refuse Him who speaks. For if they [the Israelites] did not escape when they refused the one on earth [Moses] who instructed them, much less *shall* we *escape* who turn away from the One from heaven [Christ]" (Heb. 12:25). Waiting for the Spirit to declare a man to be born again is our only means of escape from the confusion and uncertainty which results from relying on human testimonies.

Two Witnesses

Jesus said to the Jews, "In *your* law it is written that the testimony of two men is true. I'm one who bears witness of myself, and the Father who sent me bears witness of me" (Jn. 8:17–18). Two witnesses have always been required in order to establish the most important matters among the saints (e.g., Dt. 17:6), and surely, knowing who is a member of the body of Christ and who is not is one of life's most important issues. Man's confession of faith, being only one witness, cannot settle that issue. Jesus even said of himself, "If I testify about myself, my testimony is not true. There's another who testifies about me, and I know that the witness that He bears of me is true" (Jn. 5:31–32). If Jesus insisted that even his testimony was worthless if it was the only one he had, then surely we should humble ourselves to confess the same about ours.

What anyone claims about his standing with God counts for nothing. A second witness is required: the sound of the Spirit. And when the Spirit comes in and moves a person to make that sound, we may know with certainty that God has adopted that person into His holy family. The precious testimony of the Spirit, purchased for us by the blood of Christ, together with the voice of the person into whom the Spirit has come, make up the two witnesses required by God for the great matter of the new birth to be confirmed.

THE SPIRIT'S VOICE

When Nicodemus came to Jesus by night, the power of Jesus' comment about the necessity of him being "born again" stunned him. And as Nicodemus sank in heavy contemplation, Jesus went on to describe the new birth experience in these mysterious words: "The wind blows wherever it will, and you hear its sound, but you don't know where it's coming from or where it's going. So is everyone who is born of the Spirit" (Jn. 3:8). Because the Greek word for *wind* is also the word for *spirit*, a simple translation, without any manipulation whatsoever of the Greek, could be as follows: "The Spirit breathes where it will, and you hear its voice, but you cannot tell where it is coming from or where it is going. So is everyone who is born of the Spirit."

What Jesus said is critical information concerning who is really a child of God and who is not. We know that we can trust what Jesus said on this (and every other) subject, and the revelation he gave to Nicodemus is vital; it is exactly the kind of information that can unite us in a common knowledge of the truth. With that statement, Jesus revealed three fundamental truths concerning conversion, or being "born again". Let us carefully consider each of them.

"The wind blows wherever it will, and you hear its sound,
but you don't know where it's coming from or where it's going.
So is everyone who is born of the Spirit."

First, at the end of the verse, Jesus said his description of the new birth applies to *every person* born of the Spirit. This is of supreme import, for what is described by the Lord has nothing to do with what men claim. Rather, Jesus is telling what God does every time someone is born of His Spirit, without exception. This means that the Son of God has given us a way to recognize the new birth *every time it happens*!

Second, from the middle of the verse, Jesus confirms that the Spirit moves independently of men's minds, that is, man does not know where the wind of God has been nor where it will go. That is to say, man does not know who on earth was last touched by the Spirit or who it will touch next.

Third, at the beginning of John 3:8, Jesus reveals the one characteristic of being born of the Spirit that is present in every case: "The wind blows where it will, and you hear its sound." Or, "The Spirit breathes where it will, and you hear its voice."

Now, it is not as important to know that *a* sound is heard when a person is born again as it is to know that it is the Spirit that is producing the sound. The Spirit's sound is not that of a person claiming to be born again. Man's testimony concerning himself is worthless. Moreover, God has never ordained a minister, or the Bible, or even an angel from heaven to declare someone to be born again. He has reserved that honor to Himself. The Lord Jesus said that the Spirit would produce the sound. In every case, he said, "You hear its voice." A good question for all of us to ask ourselves is, "Who told me that I was born again?" Jesus said that whenever anyone is truly born again, it is the voice of the Spirit that proves it to be so. "So is EVERYONE who is born of the Spirit."

STOP JUDGING

Jesus' command, "Stop judging, so that *you* won't be judged" (Mt. 7:1), means that we must not judge others to be *right* with God as much as it means not to judge them to be otherwise. In our time, believers often judge people to be born again, even though the Spirit has not given its witness, as often as they judge people to be sinners. Yet, it is equally as wrong to judge people to be justified with God as it is to condemn them. Judging is judging, and Jesus said not to do it. Before judging someone to be born again, then, should we not wait for God's Spirit to confirm it?

In the earliest years of this covenant, the Jews who believed considered all Gentiles to be unclean just because they were Gentiles, but in Acts 10, God surprised Peter and his fellow Jews by baptizing a group of Gentiles with the Spirit. "And those of the circumcision who believed, as many as came with Peter, were astonished because the gift of the holy Spirit had also been poured out on the Gentiles! *They knew this* because they heard them speaking in tongues and magnifying God" (Acts 10:45–46a). Peter was beginning to understand that with God, righteousness is a matter of the heart, not a matter of which nation one belonged to. When Peter returned to Jerusalem, he was criticized by some Jewish believers for going to a Gentile's house, but Peter explained to them that God had sent him to preach to those

Gentiles and that as he was preaching, "the holy Spirit fell on them just as on us at the beginning. Inasmuch, then, as God gave them the same gift *He gave* to us who believed on the Lord Jesus Christ, who was I, that I could withstand God?" (Acts 11:15, 17). Later, he again had to explain to Jewish believers what God had done: "God, who knows the heart, bore them witness, giving them the holy Spirit just as *He gave it* to us, and He made no distinction between us and them, purifying their hearts by faith" (Acts 15:8–9).

The making of any judgment apart from the Spirit of truth is dangerous. If the Spirit was sent to guide us into *all* truth (Jn. 16:13), then what truth may be obtained without it? And can it be too much for God to expect that we wait for the sound of the Spirit to let us know that someone has been born again, when the sign was provided so that we *would* wait for it?

THE CRY OF BIRTH

Paul described the sound of God's Spirit when it enters into a heart in terms of the birth cry of a newborn baby. Paul's comment to the Galatians stands out: "Because *you* are sons, God sent forth the Spirit of His Son into *your* hearts, crying, 'Abba!' (*that is*, 'Father!')" (Gal. 4:6). Again, it is the Spirit's cry, not man's, that is emphasized. To the assembly of saints at Rome, Paul wrote the same: "*You* did not receive a spirit of slavery, leading back into fear, but *you* received the Spirit of adoption, by which we cry out, 'Abba!' (*that is*, 'Father!'). The Spirit itself bears witness, together with our spirit, that we are the children of God" (Rom. 8:15–16). The clear sense of these two scriptures is that the sound which indicates that one has been born into God's kingdom is a sound beyond the powers of mortal man to produce by himself. It is true, as Paul said, that "we cry out," but it is also true that the holy Spirit is the means "by which" we do so.

The Greek verb *kratzo* is the word translated "cry out" in the above verses, and it signifies a fervent verbal expression. *Kratzo* is used approximately sixty times in the New Testament books, and in every case, it is used to denote an actual vocalization, usually the result of a circumstance overwhelming the speaker's being. Some examples are: demons "cry out" when face-to-face with Jesus' powerful presence (e.g., Mt. 8:29; Mk. 3:11; Lk. 4:41); Jesus' death scream on the cross was a "crying out" (Mt. 27:50); and desperate individuals, such as Bartimaeus (Mk. 10:46f) and the Syro-Phoenician woman, "cried out" for deliverance when Jesus passed by (Mk. 7:25f). This makes it clear that the "cry" of the Spirit at a new birth is not an internal thing, heard by no one. The original readers of Paul's messages would never have understood his reference to the Spirit's "crying out" to be a private, internal event. The word *kratzo* never signified that. They would have understood perfectly that Paul was referring to the same spiritual experience that Jesus described to Nicodemus when he said, "The wind blows wherever it will, . . . and you hear its sound. So is everyone who is born of the Spirit."

Here is a testimony from Brother Tim Sellers concerning what Jesus said to Nicodemus:

In the fall of 1985, I began seeking the Lord with my whole heart and repenting of things that Jesus would put on my heart to make right. As a result of that, I received the holy Ghost baptism. That experience came with the sound of a new language, speaking in tongues. Bess, the girl I would soon marry, also received the baptism of the holy Ghost not many days after I did, also with the evidence of speaking in tongues. This was an incredible time for us as we found ourselves desiring to live a holy life.

We attended different church denominations through the next several years, all the while wanting to learn more about walking by the Spirit, and in 1994, we ended up in a charismatic church. At the time, I worked for a company that participated in our local power company's residential home programs. One of the leads given to me by them in 1996 was Bob and Ellen Payne. As I drove to the appointment, the Lord let me know it was not by accident that I was going to their house. While I was there, the conversation turned towards the things of the Spirit, and the question of the difference between salvation and the new birth experience came up, with Ellen giving me a cassette tape teaching series on the new birth by John Clark, Sr., who was their pastor.

The charismatic church that we were attending was a Word of Faith church started by Kenneth Hagin. He also had a tape series on receiving the holy Spirit that I had listened to many times, but there were gaps in his teaching that left me with more questions than answers. The big question in my heart was, are salvation and the new birth different experiences? This was my opportunity to listen to the teaching series that I just received from Ellen to compare it with Kenneth Hagin's holy Spirit series.

We had two cassette tape players, so I had the thought to put one cassette from Kenneth Hagin's series in one player and one of John Clark's cassettes in the second player. I would listen for several minutes to one, then I would pause it and listen to the other player for a few minutes. This went on for hours as I went through the cassettes in the two series. What I realized was that Kenneth Hagin would begin telling a story just before it was time to explain what happened as a person was born again, and then he would skip over that explanation (the most important part!) and pick up on the other side of their new birth experience, saying that the person had been born again. I listened very closely to his words, but still felt unclear as to what he was really saying. But when I listened to John Clark tell about the new birth experience, he did not skip over the actual experience itself. On the contrary, he gave scriptures from John 3 where Jesus was talking with Nicodemus about being born again. There, Jesus described the wind (of the Spirit) blowing where it will, and he said that you would hear a sound from the Spirit at the moment of the new birth.

After laboring through the process of listening to these two cassette series for hours, I hit the stop button on the cassette players and paused for a moment. I asked Jesus to teach me who was telling the truth. Then, I heard the Spirit ask me a question:

"What were you listening for?" At that moment, I knew exactly what He was asking me. I did not have to scratch my head and wonder what He was talking about because my thoughts went back to when my wife was pregnant with our first baby about a year before this time. Bess had to have an emergency c-section, and as she was in the operating room, I was pacing outside in the hallway talking to Jesus. I told Jesus that if I could just hear the cry of the baby, I would know he was alive. That's when I heard the Spirit say, "That's what I'm listening for, too [at the new birth experience]." With that answer from Jesus, I knew who was telling the truth about when a person is born again! There is always a sound that the Father is listening for as a new baby is being born into the body of Christ, and it is present every time a person receives the Spirit of God.

"EVERY SPIRIT THAT CONFESSES"

Isaiah prophesied that when the Messiah came, "He will not judge by what his eyes see, nor will he make decisions by what his ears hear," but "in righteousness will he judge" (Isa. 11:3–4a). And Jesus told his disciples that they were to do the same: "Do not judge by appearances, but judge righteous judgment!" (Jn. 7:24). Considering Jesus' refusal to make any judgment based on human testimony or action (cf. Isa. 11:3b), it is unthinkable that his apostles would have done differently. What John taught about how to tell when someone receives the Spirit of God is, along with Jesus' words to Nicodemus, among the most important in the Bible. He wrote, "By this, the Spirit of God is known:[1] every spirit that confesses Jesus Christ when he has come into a person is of God" (1Jn. 4:2).

It is fundamental to the understanding of this passage of Scripture to note that John was speaking of the confession of the Spirit, not the confession of humans. Many Christian translators of the New Testament actually change John's words to make it

---

[1] The United Bible Societies' Greek text has, "By this, *you* know the Spirit of God".

seem that he is talking about human confession, but that is only because they do not understand what John was saying. John knew better than to think that a person who admits that Jesus lived in the flesh has the Spirit of God within him. What John was really teaching is that every time the Spirit of God enters a fleshly temple of a man, the Spirit confesses that Jesus Christ has come in. And with that, John's teaching reflects that of Jesus, who told John and the other disciples, "When the Comforter comes . . . he will testify of me" (Jn. 15:26).

When John wrote, "Whoever confesses that Jesus is the Son of God, God abides in him, and he in God" (1Jn. 4:15), John's readers knew that he was speaking of a confession which can only be made when a person is moved by the Spirit of God to make it. Jesus had warned John and his other disciples not to be fooled by what men say or appear to be (cf. Mt. 7:15; Lk. 21:8), and in light of that, it is inconceivable that John would teach that whoever says that Jesus is God's Son is born again. The apostles were wise enough to know that the spirits of greed (1Pet. 5:2; 2Pet. 2:3; Jude 1:11–19) or pride (3Jn. 1:9) or deceit (2Cor. 11:13–15) or even the spirits of envy and strife (Phip. 1:15–16) could motivate someone to admit that Jesus is the Son of God.

After John himself was born again, he came to understand that it is the Spirit that bears witness "because the Spirit is truth" (1Jn. 5:6c). To bear witness, as meant here by John, is not possible without the Spirit, and all the apostles knew that. As Paul said it, "No one speaking by the Spirit of God is saying, 'Jesus is accursed.' And no one can say, 'Jesus is Lord', but by the holy Spirit" (1Cor. 12:3). Thus, Paul taught precisely what Jesus and John taught, namely, that the Spirit of God is the true confessor of Christ and that men may participate in that holy confession only as they participate in the life of the Spirit.

The Anti-Christ Spirit

The rest of John's message concerning how to tell the real Spirit of God from a false one is also important. This was his whole message: "By this, the Spirit of God is known: every spirit that confesses Jesus Christ when he has come into a person is of God, and every spirit that does not confess Jesus Christ when he has come into a person is not of God. And this is that of the anti-Christ which *you* have heard is coming, and now, already, it is in the world" (1Jn. 4:2–3). John is saying plainly that any spirit that does not come in with the sign of a sound is not of God. In other words, when there is no sign from God – when there is no second witness – and people can only claim to have received the Spirit of God, it is unwise to believe them, for the real Spirit always produces a sound when it enters a heart, as Jesus said: "So is everyone who is born of the Spirit."

Dear Friend, if you have been persuaded to believe you have the Spirit of God, yet God has not given His sign that you have done so, do not be discouraged. You can escape that anti-Christ spirit by trusting in the living Word of God rather than in the words of men. Seek the Lord now, while he may be found; call upon him while he is near. The door is still open!

THE MOST UNRULY MEMBER

James said that although men have tamed virtually every species of animal on earth, no man can tame his own tongue. "The tongue is a fire," James wrote, "a world of unrighteousness. The tongue is so situated among our members that it defiles the whole body and sets on fire the wheel of life, and it is set on fire by Gehenna.[2] No one among men can tame the tongue; it is an uncontrollable evil, full of deadly poison" (Jas. 3:6, 8). Because the tongue is the body's most unruly member, only when a man completely surrenders his heart to God can his tongue finally be tamed.

This taming of the tongue, demonstrated by the Spirit's control of it, is the surest indication that the Lord has become

---

[2] The word *Gehenna* is often mistranslated as "hell", but it actually refers to what John called in Revelation "the Lake of Fire". See *What the Bible Really Says about Hell*, available for online reading at GoingtoJesus.com.

Master of the heart, for the tongue and the heart have a unique relationship. Jesus revealed that relationship when he said, "Out of the abundance of the heart, the mouth speaks" (Mt. 12:34). That is always the case, whether for good or bad. Whenever the Spirit of God sanctifies and fills a heart, the tongue is always moved to express it. This explains why, whenever Christ circumcises a heart from its corrupt nature, the tongue cries out to God, "Father!" This is a glorious experience, one greatly to be desired, for when God's glory fills a repentant heart and the rebellious tongue is tamed, it is not a painful surrender. The Psalmist summed it up beautifully when he said, "My heart was glad, and my tongue rejoiced!" (Acts 2:26; cf. Ps. 16:9).

THE SEED

Before Christ came, the children of Abraham were those who were descended from his physical seed, and God chose as the sign of His covenant with Abraham the circumcision of that part of the body through which man's seed passes. This circumcision was no small matter with God. When He made His covenant with Abraham, He said, "This is my covenant, which *you* shall keep between me and *you*, and your children after you: Every male among *you* is to be circumcised. *You* are to be circumcised in the flesh of *your* foreskin, and it will be for a sign of the covenant between me and *you*. . . . An uncircumcised male who is not circumcised . . . shall certainly be cut off from his people. He has broken my covenant" (Gen. 17:10–11, 14). And after Abraham's seed became the nation of Israel, God commanded Israel to continue His covenant with Abraham and to cast out any male who was not circumcised.

In this covenant, "the seed is the word of God" (Lk. 8:11), not the seed of a man. The children of Abraham are now those with faith in Christ (Gal. 3:14, 22), who are born "not of corruptible [physical] seed but of incorruptible, by the living and eternally enduring word of God" (1Pet. 1:23). This is the revelation which prompted Paul's bold statement that "one is not a Jew outwardly;

nor is circumcision outward in the flesh. But one is a Jew inwardly, and circumcision is of the heart, by the Spirit" (Rom. 2:28–29). And the tongue, which is the body part through which the incorruptible word of God comes, partakes of circumcision with the heart and declares it, "as the Spirit moves them to speak."

In this covenant, circumcision, being spiritual, is required of both men and women. And just as it was under the Old Covenant, it is unwise to refuse God's offer of circumcision, for circumcision is the door into covenant with God. Paul rejoiced in that: "We are the circumcision," he wrote, "who serve God in spirit, and rejoice in Christ Jesus, and put no confidence in the flesh" (Phil. 3:3). This is the new "Israel of God" (Gal. 6:16), the holy nation that was born in one day (Isa. 66:8) – the day that Jesus offered himself to God for our sins and his disciples "were all filled with holy Spirit, and they began to speak in other tongues as the Spirit moved them to speak" (Acts 2:4).

Calling on the Name of the Lord

It is true that the Scriptures say that "whoever shall call upon the name of the Lord shall be saved" (Joel 2:32; Rom. 10:13), but what does the Bible mean by the phrase "calling on the name of the Lord"? In many scriptures, that phrase is connected with the worship of God's people, an example being Psalm 116:17: "I will offer to you a sacrifice of thanksgiving, and on the name of the LORD will I call." This act of worship is not possible for sinners. In fact, the definition of a sinner is a person who does not call on the name of the Lord: "Pour out your wrath on the nations that do not know you, and on the kingdoms that do not call on your name" (Ps. 79:6). The "workers of iniquity", wrote David, are they who "do not call on the LORD" (Ps. 14:4). "But as for me," he said later, "I will call on God, and the LORD will save me" (Ps. 55:16).

Paul asked this rhetorical question: "How shall they call on him in whom they have not believed?" (Rom. 10:14). The answer is they cannot. One must be a believer in order to be able to do what the Bible refers to as "calling on the name of the Lord". Calling on the name of the Lord is an experience possible only for those whose prayers are sanctified so that they may reach the ear of God. The prophet Zephaniah said that to call on the name of the Lord would be made possible only when God granted to men "a pure language", which is a clear reference to the Pentecostal experience: "At that time, I will turn to the nations a pure language so that they may all call on the name of the LORD, to serve Him in one accord" (Zeph. 3:9).

When Jesus said (Jn. 10:10), "I am come that they might have life," he was referring to the Spirit of God, for it is the Spirit which makes men truly alive (Jn. 6:63) because the Spirit is life (Rom. 8:10). From this, we can see that when David was moved by the Spirit to pray to God, "Give us life, and we will call on your name" (Ps. 80:18), he was praying for us all, as a prophet, for the Spirit to come so that we could call on the name of the Lord, a prayer that was answered a thousand years later in Acts 2. In Psalm 51, David was again moved by the Spirit to plead for the Spirit to come: "My Lord, open my lips, and my mouth will make your praise known" (Ps. 51:15). How David would have loved to have been there when the Spirit came and "opened the lips" of Jesus' disciples and gave them power to call on God in the "new and living way" of this covenant!

WHO NEEDS IT?

If a sound made by the Spirit through a person is God's evidence that He has baptized that person with His Spirit, then who needs to hear that sound, besides the one who receives it? God certainly needs no evidence; He knows all things. Who, then, needs to have proof that the Spirit has been received? Who needs to know who really has God's Spirit and who does not? Certainly, unbelievers have that need. In Paul's words, "Tongues are for a sign, not to those who believe, but to those who do not believe" (1Cor. 14:22a). One of the greatest proofs of God's love for sinners is that He has given them a sure, consistent sign to indicate the way to His mercy, if they want it.

But since tongues are God's sign for unbelievers, one should ask, "A sign of what?" Isaiah gave us the answer when he prophesied that the Spirit speaking through someone would be God Himself speaking to the disobedient, showing them where they can find rest from sin: "He will speak to this people with stammering lips and another tongue, to whom He said, 'This is the rest with which *you* will cause the weary one to rest,' and, 'This is the refreshing'" (Isa. 28:11–12a).

In 1977, I pointed out to a professor of mine at Oral Roberts University that the apostle Paul said that when Isaiah spoke of "stammering lips and another tongue", he was prophesying about speaking in tongues (1Cor. 14:21–22). The professor smiled condescendingly and said, "Paul might not have understood the Old Testament as well as he might have." Irritated by his arrogant response, I replied, "You might not have understood Paul as well as you might have." My belief then, as it is now, is that if a man has to condemn the apostle Paul in order to justify his own doctrine, neither that man nor his doctrine is worthy of much esteem.

People all over the world, in every religion, declare the holiness, goodness, and power of God. But the attributing of glory to God does not, for the sinner seeking God, distinguish the true faith from the many false ones. Men can claim anything, but the baptism of the holy Ghost is unique; it comes from God only in the name of His Son Jesus, not in the name of Muhammed or Buddha, or anyone else. It is the essential experience in the true way of eternal life. All four of the gospels record John the Baptist proclaiming that the baptism of the Spirit would be the prime credential of the Christ (cf. Mt. 3:11; Mk. 1:8; Lk. 3:16; Jn. 1:32–33), a baptism confirmed for man by the Father's sign: the Spirit's sound.

Many Pentecostals are adamant that the initial evidence of the baptism of Christ is speaking in tongues, and that alone; but that position is too narrow to embrace all that is meant by a "sound".

To demand that everyone who is baptized with the Spirit speaks in a clear language can damage souls who have received the Spirit without doing so.   One man visited our prayer meeting who had been told for years by his congregation that he had not received the Spirit, even though when he prayed, he had often made a sound through trembling lips.   He struggled on, spiritually, disappointed that he was not yet born again because he had not yet spoken in a clear language.   But when I explained to him that Jesus said only that the Spirit would make a sound and that Isaiah included "stammering lips" as one of the sounds the Spirit might make, his whole world was set aright, and he found relief in that.   The sound of the Spirit brings about a feeling that nothing can imitate.   I have watched videos of God's people on different continents worshipping Him in spirit – secret gatherings in China, congregations in Africa, and so forth – and the feeling aroused by the sound of their praise in the Spirit was as familiar and sweet to me as when my own congregation is caught up in the worship of God.

What kind of audible confirmation the Spirit gives at Spirit baptism is up to God, not man, and because it is of God and not man, any religion without that sound must be false, regardless of what that religion calls itself, be it Islam, Hinduism, or even Christianity.   What men call anything is irrelevant; it is the sound of the Spirit that confirms that one has entered into covenant with God.

As long as there is hope for unbelievers, there will be a need for the Spirit's sound at Spirit baptism.   It is only when "that which is perfect is come" and the Final Judgment on mankind has been made that the Spirit's sound will cease (cf. 1Cor. 13:8–10).   No one at that time will need a witness from God to let him know who is a believer, for believers will be the only ones left standing.   But as yet, there remains a need for God to help the thirsty to find the waters of life.

In this, the mighty care of God for man is revealed, that in a world filled with human voices claiming to be teaching the way to eternal life, God Himself actually condescends to speak through every true believer, declaring to every confused and hungry soul, "This is the way; walk in it." It is the purest love and wisdom of God, that He should begin each believer's spiritual life with a divinely inspired testimony for the sake of those looking for the truth!

Thankfully, God has not left us on our own to determine which way is right. He calls from heart to heart, not with reasons but with feelings stirred up by a sound. When God's Spirit fills someone to overflowing, and the Spirit's voice is heard, the sinner is called upon for a decision – a decision that is of the heart, not the head. It is the depth of God's soul reaching out to the depth of man's soul, as David said, "Deep calls to deep at the sound of your waterspouts" (Ps. 42:7a).

REST FOR THE WEARY

My father had a dream in which he was burying the Lord after his crucifixion. Just as he was about to lower him into the grave, Jesus opened his eyes, and raising both his hands, he said to my father, "Here, this cannot be buried with me."

My father then saw in one hand twenty-eight dollars and eleven cents and in the other, eleven dollars and twenty-eight cents. He reached and took the money, as Jesus had instructed him, and as he looked at the money, it changed into two books of the Bible. The twenty-eight dollars and eleven cents became Isaiah, and the eleven dollars and twenty-eight cents became Matthew. Here is the verse from Matthew: "Come to me, all who labor and are heavily laden, and <u>I will give you rest</u>" (Mt. 11:28). And from Isaiah 28:11: "With stammering lips and another tongue He will speak to this people." In the very next verse, Isaiah says, "To whom He said, '<u>This is the rest</u> with which you will cause the weary one to rest,' and, 'This is the refreshing.'"

In the holy Spirit, Jesus offers us rest from sin and shame. But the Son of God's ancient question can still be asked: "Who has believed our report?" (Isa. 53:1). For God has chosen "the foolishness of preaching, to save those who believe" (1Cor. 1:21). And "God has chosen the foolish things of the world, that He might put the wise to shame" and "things that are despised [such as being moved to speak by the invisible Spirit of God], and the things that are not, that He might bring to nothing the things that are" (1Cor. 1:27–28). God has purposely designed this New Covenant so that only the humble will believe the gospel and receive the holy rest that Jesus gives.

"The foolishness of God is wiser than men," wrote Paul, and God's magnificent "foolishness" in choosing the sound of the Spirit as the sign of the new birth is revealed, in part, by the fact that proud people are ashamed to be seen yielding to the Spirit. Self-willed people refuse to yield their hearts (and, so, their tongues) to the Spirit. So, establishing the lowly standard of giving voice to the Spirit at Spirit baptism has proved to be God's wise way of keeping the ungodly from even wanting to be in His kingdom. Seeing that the proudest souls are often the most highly regarded and powerful among men, Paul wrote, "You see your calling, brothers, that not many wise in the flesh, not many powerful, not many of noble birth, are called" (1Cor. 1:26a).

Because of what Jesus described as "the deceitfulness of riches", wealthy people often are too proud to repent and receive the holy Spirit. Jesus said it was easier for a camel to go through the eye of a needle than for a rich man to enter the kingdom of God (Mt. 19:24). James said that God has chosen the poor instead of the rich to receive His favor (Jas. 2:5). The kingdom of God is for the poor in spirit, and undeniably, the poor in spirit are, in great measure, also the poor in this world's goods.

CONVERSATIONS

Some years ago, a Church of God minister, a friend of mine named Lee, mentioned to me his church's position, that one must believe and "get saved" before being baptized with the Spirit. I replied, "But Lee, that's the opposite of what Jesus taught. Jesus said, 'He who believes and is baptized will be saved,' not, 'He who believes and gets saved shall be baptized.' Somebody has it backwards." Lee promised he would get back with me after reviewing the Church of God Minute Book, but unfortunately, he moved out of town and passed away before we had that discussion.

In 1979, in a letter sent to me from a prince in the kingdom of God, Oral Roberts (to whom I owe my life for healing my dying father before I was born), Brother Roberts put forth the same position as my friend Lee. Rather than summarize his remarks and run the risk of misrepresenting this great man of God, I will reproduce his letter in full:

Oral Roberts
April 27, 1979

Dear John:

I appreciate you writing me back and sharing some of the thoughts you have concerning the baptism of the Holy Spirit. I can tell you are struggling with this. And while I don't have time enough to answer each of the points you shared, I do feel impressed to share a thought with you that may help you.

John, your main concern seems to be that a person's conversion doesn't really take place until the moment they are baptized with the Holy Spirit. Now, I firmly believe that the Holy Spirit is in you when you first come to the Lord. Indeed, it is the Holy Spirit Who draws you to God. But the Scripture indicates there is a deeper dimension of the Holy Spirit that is available to those who believe on Jesus. And that is the baptism with the Holy Spirit.

Focus your attention now on John 3:16. It says that God so loved the world He gave His only begotten Son so that who-soever believed on Him would have everlasting life. Now, who did God love? He loved the world — the world and everyone in it, everyone from that generation to this and everyone yet to be born until the Second Coming of Christ. Also, the promise of everlasting life (the promise of salvation) is given to whosoever believes on Jesus. TO

WHOSOEVER. There is no special qualification given here. Salvation is promised to anyone in the world who believes on Jesus.

Now look at I Corinthians 2:11-16. Read it carefully, paying attention to these words – "Now we have received, not the spirit of the world, but the spirit which is of God . . . but the natural man receiveth not the things of the Spirit of God: for they are foolishness to him . . ." You see, there is a separation point concerning the baptism with the Holy Spirit. While salvation is freely given to the world, this baptism is reserved for those who have chosen to join the body of Christ. It can come to them at any time after they have believed on Jesus, but at no time before.

I hope this helps clarify what I teach about the Holy Spirit. Feel free to write me at any time. Now, God bless you in every way.

(Signed) Oral Roberts

I read this letter at least twice, and yet, I could not understand it. I bowed my head and prayed, and I earnestly asked God what this holy man, whom I loved so much, was trying to get across to me, but I still could not understand his words. Finally, I carried the letter to my elderly father and asked him to read it and explain it to me. He put on his reading glasses and read it in silence. Then, in a meek voice, he summed it up in one sentence. "He's saying that salvation is for sinners and the baptism of the Spirit is for saints." Then I saw that the reason I had not been able to understand what Brother Roberts had written was that he was using the word "salvation" as a synonym for "conversion", which is a confusing error.

Brother Roberts' letter was saying that one must be born again before one can receive the holy Spirit baptism. I had hoped for more. That doctrine is typical of Pentecostals and Charismatics everywhere, though it is biblically indefensible. There is not one example in the New Testament of someone being born again and later being baptized with the holy Ghost. In the Scriptures, the method of conversion is this: people heard the gospel of Christ, felt conviction for their sins and repented, and then received the baptism of the Spirit. No one was ever born again before receiving that baptism.

By that time in my life, I had also learned that there is no such thing as a man choosing "to join the body of Christ"; yet, Brother Roberts said the baptism of the holy Ghost was reserved for those who had done that. Paul stated plainly that we are baptized by the Spirit into the body of Christ (1Cor. 12:13); how then could the baptism be reserved for people who had joined it? Joining something is an act of man's will, but is there anything in the kingdom of God that is accomplished by the will of man? Granting the new birth is an act of God's will, and John said that those who believe "are born, not of blood, nor of the will of the flesh, nor of the will of man, but of God" (Jn. 1:13).

As for the word *salvation*, the apostles and the Lord Jesus, unlike Brother Roberts and many other ministers, most often referred to salvation as the reward Jesus will give to faithful saints when he returns. Biblically speaking, salvation is best understood as a synonym for glorification, which will not happen until after this life has been lived. Contrary to what Brother Roberts taught, salvation is not offered to sinners. To receive salvation, sinners must first repent and stop being sinners, be baptized by the Spirit into the body of Christ, and then live in holiness until the end. As Jesus said, "He who endures to the end, the same shall be saved" (Mt. 24:13).

Again, contrary to the teaching of Brother Roberts and others, Jesus' apostles proclaimed the baptism of the Spirit to be for sinners who would believe the gospel and repent. The baptism of the holy Ghost is the very thing that washes away the sinner's sin and gives him the hope of the salvation to come (cf. 1Pet. 3:21; Tit. 3:5). Paul's conversion and cleansing from sin, for example, took place in the city of Damascus, when he was baptized with the Spirit (Acts 22:11, 16), not when he was on the way there to arrest those who called on the name of the Lord (cf. Acts 9:14).

How could such a great man of God as Oral Roberts not have seen that? That was a deeply disturbing mystery that I cannot yet fathom. It has vexed my spirit many times over the years as I pondered over how an anointed man of God such as he could think that the baptism of the holy Ghost can be received only after conversion when all the biblical evidence shows that the baptism of the Spirit *is* conversion! That question troubled my spirit so badly, not because I thought I was closer to God than Brother Roberts, but because I knew that he was closer to God than I. It was because I honored him so highly that my heart was grieved that I could not agree with him on this fundamental issue. But when I tried to read the Bible as he read it concerning the baptism of the Spirit, it was impossible for me to make him right. It was almost maddening. I wanted to be wrong; I ached inside to find my error; I tried to make the Bible say what he said so that I could agree with him, but the Scriptures just would not yield themselves to it.

"It's Like Facing a Hurricane"

I am part of a small minority of believers who teach that the baptism of the holy Ghost, with the accompanying sound of the Spirit, is the experience Jesus described to Nicodemus as being born again. But what is to be done? The numbers against us and the great names who contradict us are formidable. Many traditions and doctrines that oppose us are set in stone, so to speak, and have been revered by millions for many centuries. As my father once put it, "It's like standing outside facing a hurricane, trying to blow it back where it came from."

I am fully aware of the ramifications of what I am teaching, ramifications so great that, understandably, they make reasonable men pause. Still, if what Jesus said is true, if every time a person is baptized with the Spirit, the Spirit's voice is heard, then the only biblically sound conclusion is that no one is born again unless he has received the Spirit and the Spirit has spoken through him, whether in a language, or with the "groaning" Paul mentioned, or with some other sound. That is what Jesus said would happen every time someone is born of the Spirit.

God help me. Here I stand. I cannot see it any other way, though God knows how sincerely I have tried.

CONCLUSION

This booklet presents the most accurate and consistent biblical explanation I can find for the sound of the Spirit being the sign that one has been baptized by Christ with the holy Spirit. This doctrine, taken to its logical conclusion, alters radically the commonly accepted picture of the body of Christ. For, since the baptism of the Spirit is the means of entering the body of Christ (1Cor. 12:13), the body of Christ is composed exclusively of those who have received the Spirit, with the audible evidence that Jesus said would accompany that blessing.

Paul said that "if anyone does not have the Spirit of Christ, he does not belong to him" (Rom. 8:9), and it is absolutely necessary for God's children to know who has received the Spirit and who has not. Otherwise, we are lost in a world of confusion as to who really belongs to God and who does not, which is precisely the situation among believers today. The signs that Christians put forth as evidence that someone has been born again are many and contradictory – showing love, or demonstrating sincere belief, or characteristics akin to the fruit of the Spirit being most often mentioned. But they are all based on human judgment and/or someone's understanding of the Scriptures. The sound of the Spirit is the only sign that can be trusted because it is the only sign of the new birth that God has given.

Having been taught that the baptism of the Spirit is only for some in the body of Christ, Pentecostals are tempted to think that those who are baptized with the Spirit are the spiritually mature in the body. But when we are baptized with the Spirit, we have merely become newborns in Christ. Non-Pentecostals, on the other hand, should be cautioned that we are never told to "take it by faith" that we have received the Spirit. Rather, we "receive the promise of the Spirit through faith" (Gal. 3:14), and when the Spirit comes, as Jesus and his apostles taught, it testifies. Being baptized with the holy Ghost has never been something we must assume has happened based on a doctrine we have been taught or on a scripture that someone interprets for us. Rather, it is an experience that we receive because we believe the gospel and repent.

God's acceptance of Abel's offering angered Cain so much that he murdered his brother rather than amend his evil ways so that his offering would also be acceptable. God told Cain that he need not be angry, for if he did what was right, he, too, would be accepted. But rather than repent of his evildoing, he chose to get rid of the one whom God had accepted. Likewise, it sometimes angers people without the Spirit when God accepts the repentance of others and "bears them witness, giving them the holy Spirit". But that is only because, like Cain, God's choice has exposed them as still being sinners.

God, who alone knows the heart, always chooses rightly whom to fill and whom not to fill with His Spirit. Peter boldly told the Sanhedrin when he was on trial, "The God of our fathers raised up Jesus, whom *you* killed, hanging him on a tree. This man God has exalted to His right hand to be a Prince and a Savior, to give repentance to Israel, and forgiveness of sins. And we are his witnesses of these things, and so is the holy Spirit, which God has given to those who obey Him" (Acts 5:30–32). Those judges were so enraged at Peter's words, which exposed them as not having obeyed God, that they were determined to kill him (Acts 5:33), but being cautioned against it, they flogged him instead, and commanded him never to preach the gospel again (Acts 5:40).

Regardless of any earthly opposition that may come, whether it be contempt, slander, or cruel abuse, the sacrificed Son still sits at the Father's right hand, and because of that, the blessing of the Spirit is still available for "whosoever will". Seeing others receive that blessing should not anger but encourage whoever is without it, for "God is no respecter of persons, but in every nation, whoever fears Him and works righteousness is acceptable to Him" (Acts 10:34–35).   And when God accepts anyone and gives him His Spirit, others hear a sound.

"So is EVERYONE who is born of the Spirit."

Amen, Jesus.

Appendix

What Happens at the Moment of New Birth

The experience of being born again is so great that it cannot be fully described in a few words. Just as Jesus has many titles, such as Savior, Master, Lord, Prince of Peace, and so on, so also, the new birth which he gives is so full of meaning that it is called by many names. The following is a list of fifty things which take place the moment we are born again. All fifty, and more, take place simultaneously, in "the twinkling of an eye", when we are born of God.

1. We receive God's Spirit at the moment of new birth.

Galatians 3:13–14: In Christ Jesus, the blessing of Abraham comes to the Gentiles, namely, that we might receive the promise of the Spirit through faith.

Acts 1:4: Being assembled together with them, he commanded them not to leave Jerusalem but to await the promise of the Father, "which", he said, "you have heard about from me."

2. We are baptized with God's Spirit at the moment of new birth.

Acts 1:5: [Jesus to his disciples] "John indeed baptized with water, but you will be baptized with holy Spirit not many days from now."

3. The Spirit makes a sound through us at the moment of new birth.

John. 3:7–8: [Jesus to Nicodemus] "Do not marvel that I told you, 'You must be born again.' The wind blows wherever it will, and you hear its sound, but you don't know where it's coming from or where it's going. So is everyone who is born of the Spirit."

Romans 8:16: The Spirit itself bears witness, together with our spirit, that we are the children of God.

4. GOD BECOMES OUR FATHER AT THE MOMENT OF NEW BIRTH.

Galatians 4:6: God sent forth the Spirit of His Son into your hearts, crying, "Abba!" (that is, "Father!").

Romans 8:9b: If anyone does not have the Spirit of Christ, he does not belong to him.

5. WE BECOME CHILDREN OF GOD AT THE MOMENT OF NEW BIRTH.

1 John 3:1: What great love the Father has bestowed on us, that we should be called children of God! The reason the world does not know you is that it did not know Him.

6. WE ARE ADOPTED INTO THE FAMILY OF GOD AT THE MOMENT OF NEW BIRTH.

Romans 8:15: You received the Spirit of adoption, by which we cry out, "Abba!" (that is, "Father!").

7. WE ARE MADE JOINT-HEIRS WITH CHRIST AT THE MOMENT OF NEW BIRTH.

Romans 8:16–17: The Spirit itself bears witness, together with our spirit, that we are the children of God, and if children, then heirs — heirs of God, and heirs with Christ.

8. WE ARE MADE NEW CREATURES AT THE MOMENT OF NEW BIRTH.

2 Corinthians 5:17a: If anyone be in Christ, he is a new creature.

9. WE ARE GIVEN A NEW PAST AT THE MOMENT OF NEW BIRTH.

2 Corinthians 5:17b: Old things are gone; behold, all things are new.

10. CHRIST AND THE FATHER ENTER INTO US AT THE MOMENT OF NEW BIRTH.

John 14:23: [Jesus to his disciples] "If anyone loves me, he will obey my word, and my Father will love him, and we will come to him and make our home with him."

11. WE ENTER INTO CHRIST AND THE FATHER AT THE MOMENT OF NEW BIRTH.

John 17:20–21, 23a: [Jesus to God] "I am not asking for these alone, but also for those who believe in me through their word, that they all might be one, just as you, Father, are in me, and I in you, that they may also be one in us. . . . I in them, and you in me."

12. WE ARE MADE ABLE TO WORK TOGETHER WITH ALL GOD'S CHILDREN AT THE MOMENT OF NEW BIRTH.

Galatians 3:28: There is neither Jew nor Greek, neither slave nor freeman, nor male and female, for you are all one in Christ Jesus.

Zephaniah 3:9b: [God, concerning the last days] "I will turn to the nations a pure language so that they may all . . . serve Him in one accord."

13. WE ARE MADE ABLE TO CALL UPON GOD AT THE MOMENT OF NEW BIRTH.

Zephaniah 3:9a: [God, concerning the last days] "I will turn to the nations a pure language so that they may all call on the name of the LORD."

14. OUR SINS ARE WASHED AWAY AT THE MOMENT OF NEW BIRTH.

Acts 22:16: [Ananias to Saul of Tarsus] "So now, why are you waiting? Get up and be baptized, and wash away your sins, calling on the name of the Lord!"

1 Corinthians 6:11: You were washed . . . in the name of the Lord Jesus and by the Spirit of our God.

15. WE ARE CONVERTED AT THE MOMENT OF NEW BIRTH.

Matthew 18:3: [Jesus to his disciples] "Truly, I tell you, unless you are converted and become like little children, you will never enter into the kingdom of heaven."

Luke 22:32: [Jesus to Peter] "When you are converted, strengthen your brothers."

16. WE ARE REFRESHED AT THE MOMENT OF NEW BIRTH.

Isaiah 28:11–12: [God] will speak to this people with stammering lips and another tongue, to whom He said, "This is the rest with which you will cause the weary one to rest," and, "This is the refreshing."

Acts 3:19: [Peter to the Jews] "Repent and be converted, that your sins might be blotted out, so that the times of refreshing may come from the presence of the LORD!"

17. WE ARE CIRCUMCISED FROM A SINFUL NATURE AT THE MOMENT OF NEW BIRTH.

Romans 2:28–29: One is not a Jew outwardly; nor is circumcision outward in the flesh. But one is a Jew inwardly, and circumcision is of the heart, by the Spirit, not the letter, whose praise is not of men, but of God.

Colossians 2:11: You are circumcised with a circumcision per-formed without hands, in the removal of the nature of the flesh given to sins, by the circumcision of Christ.

Philippians 3:3: We are the circumcision who serve God in spirit, and rejoice in Christ Jesus, and put no confidence in the flesh.

18. WE ARE GRAFTED INTO THE VINE OF GOD AT THE MOMENT OF NEW BIRTH.

Romans 11:17: Some of the branches were broken off, and you, being a wild olive tree, were grafted in among them and have become a partaker of the root and of the fatness of the olive.

John 15:5a: [Jesus to his disciples] "I am the vine; you are the branches."

19. WE BECOME PART OF THE TRUE ISRAEL OF GOD AT THE MOMENT OF NEW BIRTH.

Galatians 6:16: As many as will conform to this rule, peace be upon them, and mercy, even upon the Israel of God.

20. WE BECOME MEMBERS OF THE BODY OF CHRIST AT THE MOMENT OF NEW BIRTH.

1 Corinthians 12:13a: By one Spirit were we all baptized into one body, whether Jews or Greeks, whether slaves or free.

21. WE ENTER INTO THE KINGDOM OF GOD AT THE MOMENT OF NEW BIRTH.

Romans 14:17: The kingdom of God is not food and drink, but righteousness and peace and joy in the holy Spirit.

22. WE ENTER INTO GOD'S NEW COVENANT AT THE MOMENT OF NEW BIRTH.

Hebrews 12:23b–24a: [Believers have come] to God, Judge of all, and to spirits of righteous people made perfect, and to the mediator of a new covenant, Jesus.

23. WE DRINK THE REAL BLOOD OF CHRIST AT THE MOMENT OF NEW BIRTH.

John 6:53–54, 63: [Jesus to his followers] "Unless you eat the flesh of the Son of man and drink his blood, you have no life in you. He who eats my flesh and drinks my blood has eternal life, and I'll raise him up on the last day. . . . It is the Spirit that gives life; the flesh profits nothing. The things that I am telling you, they are spirit, and they are life!"

1 Corinthians 12:13b: Whether Jews or Greeks, whether slaves or free, . . . all were given to drink of one Spirit.

24. WE EAT THE REAL BREAD OF CHRIST AT THE MOMENT OF NEW BIRTH.

1 Corinthians 10:17b: We, being many, are one bread, one body, for we all partake of the one bread.

John 6:48: [Jesus to a multitude] "I am the bread of life."

25. WE PARTAKE OF GOD'S DIVINE NATURE AT THE MOMENT OF NEW BIRTH.

2Peter 1:4: Precious and great promises are given to us, so that by these you might be partakers of the divine nature.

26. WE HAVE COMMUNION WITH GOD AT THE MOMENT OF NEW BIRTH.

1Corinthians 10:16: The cup of blessing that we bless, is it not the fellowship of the blood of Christ? The bread that we break, is it not the fellowship of the body of Christ?

2Corinthians 13:14: The grace of the Lord Jesus Christ, and the love of God, and the communion of the holy Spirit be with you all. Amen.

27. WE ARE REDEEMED AT THE MOMENT OF NEW BIRTH.

Titus 2:14: [The Lord Jesus] gave himself for us so that he might redeem us.

Galatians 3:13a: Christ redeemed us from the curse of the law, becoming a curse for us.

28. WE ARE SANCTIFIED AT THE MOMENT OF NEW BIRTH.

Hebrews 13:12: Jesus, that he might sanctify the people with his own blood, suffered outside the gate.

1Corinthians 6:11b: You were sanctified . . . in the name of the Lord Jesus and by the Spirit of our God.

29. WE ARE JUSTIFIED AT THE MOMENT OF NEW BIRTH.

Romans 5:9: Being now justified by his blood, we shall be saved from wrath through him.

1Corinthians 6:11c: You were justified in the name of the Lord Jesus and by the Spirit of our God.

30. WE ARE PURCHASED BY JESUS FOR GOD AT THE MOMENT OF NEW BIRTH.

1 Corinthians 6:19b–20: You are not your own, for you were bought with a price; so then, glorify God in your body, and in your spirit, which are God's.

Revelation 5:9: [The saints in heaven] sang a new song, saying, "You are worthy to take the scroll and to open its seals because you were slaughtered, and with your blood, you purchased us for God out of every tribe and tongue and people and nation."

31. WE ARE DELIVERED FROM THE REALM OF DARKNESS AT THE MOMENT OF NEW BIRTH.

Colossians 1:13: [The Father] delivered us from the domain of darkness and translated us into the kingdom of His beloved Son.

32. OUR OLD NATURE IS CRUCIFIED AT THE MOMENT OF NEW BIRTH.

Romans 6:6: Our old man is crucified with Christ so that our sinful body might be rendered powerless so that we no longer are slaves to sin.

33. WE ARE BURIED WITH CHRIST AND RISEN WITH HIM AT THE MOMENT OF NEW BIRTH.

Colossians 2:12: [You are] buried with him in baptism, in which you also are raised with him through faith in the working of God, who raised him from the dead.

34. GOD'S LAW IS WRITTEN ON OUR HEARTS AT THE MOMENT OF NEW BIRTH.

Hebrews 8:10: I will put my laws into their mind and write them on their heart, and I will be their God, and they will be my people.

35. GOD'S LOVE COMES INTO OUR HEARTS AT THE MOMENT OF NEW BIRTH.

Romans 5:5: The love of God is poured out within our hearts by the holy Spirit which is given to us.

36. WE BECOME ALIVE TO GOD AT THE MOMENT OF NEW BIRTH.

Romans 6:13b: Present yourselves to God as alive from the dead, and your members to God as instruments of righteousness.

Ephesians 2:1, 4, 5b: You were dead in transgressions and sins, but God, being rich in mercy because of His great love with which He loved us, made us alive together with Christ.

37. WE BECOME DEAD TO SIN AT THE MOMENT OF NEW BIRTH.

Romans 6:11: Think of yourselves as completely dead to sin, yet alive to God through Christ Jesus our Lord.

Romans 7:6: Having died to that by which we were bound, we are released . . . so that we now serve God in the newness of the Spirit.

38. WE BECOME WITNESSES OF GOD AT THE MOMENT OF NEW BIRTH.

Acts 1:8a: [Jesus to his disciples] "You will receive power after the holy Spirit comes upon you, and then you will be my witnesses."

39. WE BECOME "GODS" AT THE MOMENT OF NEW BIRTH.

Psalm 82:6: [God to Israel] "I have said, 'You are gods, and all of you are sons of the Most High.'"

John 10:34–35a: [Jesus to his adversaries] "Isn't it written in your law, 'I said you are gods'? [So then, God] called them 'gods' to whom the word of God came."

40. WE BECOME A CHOSEN RACE, A ROYAL PRIESTHOOD, AND A HOLY NATION BELONGING TO GOD AT THE MOMENT OF NEW BIRTH.

1Peter 2:9a: You are a chosen race, a royal priesthood, a holy nation, a people belonging to God.

41. WE BECOME LIVING STONES, USED BY JESUS TO BUILD A TEMPLE FOR THE WORSHIP OF GOD AT THE MOMENT OF NEW BIRTH.

1 Peter 2:5: You, as living stones, are being built into a spiritual house, a holy priesthood, to offer up spiritual sacrifices, acceptable to God through Jesus Christ.

42. WE BECOME THE TEMPLE OF GOD AT THE MOMENT OF NEW BIRTH.

1 Corinthians 6:19: Do you not know that your body is a temple of the holy Spirit that is in you, which you have from God?

43. WE ARE DELIVERED FROM BEING ENEMIES OF GOD AT THE MOMENT OF NEW BIRTH.

Romans 5:10a: When we were enemies, we were reconciled to God through the death of His Son.

Colossians 1:21–22a: You, who by disposition were once alienated and enemies of God with evil deeds, he has now reconciled through death in his fleshly body.

44. WE ARE DELIVERED FROM SPIRITUAL BONDAGE AT THE MOMENT OF NEW BIRTH.

Luke 4:18: [Jesus, reading Isaiah in a synagogue] "The Spirit of the LORD has sent me to heal the brokenhearted, to preach liberty to those held captive."

Galatians 4:6–7a: God sent forth the Spirit of His Son into your hearts, crying, "Abba!" (that is, "Father!"). So then, you are no longer a slave but a son.

Galatians 5:1: Therefore, stand fast in the liberty with which Christ has made us free, and do not submit again to a yoke of bondage!

45. WE ARE MADE ABLE TO CONFESS JESUS AS LORD AT THE MOMENT OF NEW BIRTH.

1 Corinthians 12:3: No one speaking by the Spirit of God is saying, "Cursed be Jesus." And no one is able to say, "Lord Jesus," but by the holy Spirit.

46. WE ARE GIVEN ACCESS TO GOD AT THE MOMENT OF NEW BIRTH.

Ephesians 2:18: Through [Jesus], we have access to the Father by one Spirit.

Hebrews 6:18b–20a: Hold fast the hope, which we have as an anchor for the soul, both secure and steadfast, and which enters into that which is within the veil, where our forerunner, Jesus, has entered for us.

47. WE ARE GIVEN A NEW HEART AT THE MOMENT OF NEW BIRTH.

Ezekiel 11:19b–20: [God to Israel] "I will take away the stony heart from their flesh, and I will give them a heart of flesh so that they may walk in my statutes and keep my judgments and do them. And they will be my people, and I will be their God."

48. WE ARE GIVEN THE MIND OF CHRIST AT THE MOMENT OF NEW BIRTH.

1 Corinthians 2:16: [It is written,] "Who has known the mind of the LORD, or who will instruct Him?" Yet, we have the mind of Christ.

49. WE ARE GIVEN HOPE OF ETERNAL LIFE AT THE MOMENT OF NEW BIRTH.

Colossians 1:27: God has willed to make known among the Gentiles what is the richness of the glory of this mystery, which is Christ in you, the hope of glory.

Ephesians. 2:12: You were at that time without Christ, having no hope, and without God in the world.

Titus 3:7: Being justified by His grace, we became heirs of the hope of eternal life.

50. WE ARE GIVEN A PROMISE OF REIGNING WITH JESUS AT THE MOMENT OF NEW BIRTH.

Romans 4:13: The promise that [Abraham] would be the heir of the world was not made to Abraham or to his seed through the law, but through the righteousness of faith.

Daniel 7:27: The sovereignty, and dominion, and greatness of the kingdoms under the whole heaven was given to the people, the saints of the Most High.

Revelation 20:4: I saw thrones, and they sat on them, and judgment was given to them, . . . and they reigned with Christ a thousand years.

AT THE MOMENT OF MY NEW BIRTH

Brother Billy Mellick said that it touched him deeply when he supplied the words, "I" and "me" for "we" and "our", and so forth, in the list of things that instantly happen the moment we are born again. Try it, and you will be blessed, too!

At the moment of my new birth, all of these things happened to ME:

1. I received God's Spirit at the moment of my new birth.
2. I was baptized with God's Spirit at the moment of my new birth.
3. The Spirit made a sound through me at the moment of my new birth.
4. God became my Father at the moment of my new birth.
5. I became a child of God at the moment of my new birth.
6. I was adopted into the family of God at the moment of my new birth.
7. I was made a joint-heir with Christ at the moment of my new birth.
8. I was made a new creature at the moment of my new birth.
9. I was given a new past at the moment of my new birth.
10. Christ and the Father entered into me at the moment of my new birth.

11. I entered into Christ and the Father at the moment of my new birth.
12. I became one with all God's children at the moment of my new birth.
13. I was made able to call upon God at the moment of my new birth.
14. My sins were washed away at the moment of my new birth.
15. I was converted at the moment of my new birth.
16. I was refreshed at the moment of my new birth.
17. I was circumcised from a sinful nature at the moment of my new birth.
18. I was grafted into the Vine of God at the moment of my new birth.
19. I became part of the true Israel of God at the moment of my new birth.
20. I became a member of the body of Christ at the moment of my new birth.
21. I entered into the kingdom of God at the moment of my new birth.
22. I entered into God's New Covenant at the moment of my new birth.
23. I drank the real blood of Christ at the moment of my new birth.
24. I ate the real bread of Christ at the moment of my new birth.
25. I partook of God's divine nature at the moment of my new birth.
26. I had communion with God at the moment of my new birth.
27. I was redeemed at the moment of my new birth.
28. I was sanctified at the moment of my new birth.
29. I was justified at the moment of my new birth.
30. I was purchased by Jesus for God at the moment of my new birth.
31. I was delivered from the realm of darkness at the moment of my new birth.
32. My old nature was crucified at the moment of my new birth.

33. I was buried with Christ and risen with him at the moment of my new birth.
34. God's law was written on my heart at the moment of my new birth.
35. God's love came into my heart at the moment of my new birth.
36. I became alive to God at the moment of my new birth.
37. I became dead to sin at the moment of my new birth.
38. I became a witness of God at the moment of my new birth.
39. I became a "god" at the moment of my new birth.
40. I became one of a chosen race, a royal priesthood, and a holy nation belonging to God at the moment of my new birth.
41. I became a living stone, used by Jesus to build a temple for the worship of God at the moment of my new birth.
42. I became the temple of God at the moment of my new birth.
43. I was delivered from being an enemy of God at the moment of my new birth.
44. I was delivered from spiritual bondage at the moment of my new birth.
45. I was made able to say that Jesus is Lord at the moment of my new birth.
46. I was given access to God at the moment of my new birth.
47. I was given a new heart at the moment of my new birth.
48. I was given the mind of Christ at the moment of my new birth.
49. I was given hope of eternal life at the moment of my new birth.
50. I was given a promise of reigning with Jesus at the moment of my new birth.

Are You Ready for Jesus Not to Come?

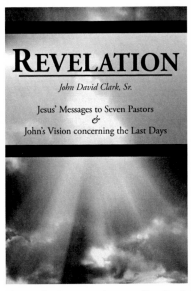

The question, "Are you ready for Jesus to come?" may be a good question to ask, but the more appropriate question is, "Are you ready for Jesus not to come?" because the reality is that it is not time for Jesus to return. So, the real issue is, are we ready to stay here and do the work that remains to be done? Are we prepared to endure what this world and the body of Christ will suffer before the coming of the Lord?

After examining the seven messages from Jesus to the pastors of seven congregations, this study of John's revelation reveals why the Jews rejected Jesus and presents in great detail the wonderful promises God made to Israel through the prophets, all of which will be fulfilled after He has greatly scourged and sifted the nation for their rebellion against Christ.

Prophet to an Apostate Nation

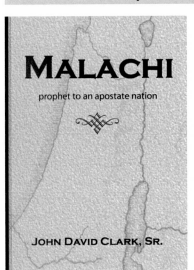

Malachi was a prophet who labored in a very dark time in Israel's history, and his answer to the darkness was the law of Moses - God's law. He pleaded with Israel to repent and live by that holy law, but the Israelites were indignant at Malachi's warnings. Ours is just such a dark time. The true word of God is rarely spoken, and when it is, it is often scorned. As the book Malachi amply shows, Jesus' comment concerning the path to eternal life, "few there be who find it," applied to ancient Israel as it does to us.

To persuade transgressors to repent and to exhort the faithful to be steadfast has been the task of God's servants throughout human history, whether they be the prophets of ancient Israel or God's ministers today. The true prophets in Israel were sent to point God's people to the way of His law, and God's true ministers today are sent to point His people to the way of His Spirit.

God Is, First of All, a God of Relationships.

God Had a Son
before Mary Did

The Significance of God's Revelation of His Son

John David Clark, Sr.

What love the Father had for us, to transform us desperately sinful creatures into saints and to re-create us as His children, worthy to live forever! God sent His Son to give us life so that we might know Him, and by revealing Himself through His Son, God accomplished the impossible in us.

The revelation that from the beginning there existed a beloved Son lets us know that above all else, God desires loving relationships. That desire lies at the heart of everything God has ever done, and nothing in Creation contradicts that truth.

God Had a Son before Mary Did examines the significance and glory of the "mystery of God", the mystery of the Son, which God kept secret from the foundation of the world until He revealed it in the person of Jesus Christ.

When Were the Disciples Born Again?

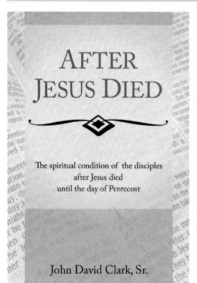

AFTER JESUS DIED

The spiritual condition of the disciples
after Jesus died
until the day of Pentecost

John David Clark, Sr.

If anyone on earth was born again after Jesus died, and before Pentecost, surely his disciples were - but they were not. If anyone on earth understood his purpose and doctrine after Jesus died, and before Pentecost, surely his disciples did - but they did not. *After Jesus Died* shows that the Bible leaves no reasonable alternative to those two conclusions.

When we carefully study the disciples' actions and words in the time between Jesus' death and the day of Pentecost, we are forced to conclude that they were not born again until they were baptized with the Spirit on Pentecost morning. May God give us the same grace that He gave to his disciples to escape spiritual blindness and to walk with Jesus in his light. "The God who commanded light to shine out of darkness has shone in our hearts to give us the light of the knowledge of the glory of God in the face of Jesus Christ."

Who Is in Charge of Our Suffering?

Let those who suffer according to the will of God commit their souls to Him in well doing, as unto a faithful Creator. 1Peter 4:19

John David Clark, Sr.

"And we know that all things work together for good to them that love God, to them who are the called according to His purpose."

Are you hurting? Have you suffered a crushing loss? We all suffer from disappointment, misunderstanding, and betrayal. What are we to think? How do we respond?

In *Suffering and the Saints,* we will read the Biblical stories of men and women whose faith survived desperate situations. But this is more than a collection of stories. We will pay close attention to what they thought about their suffering and how they perceived God's part in it. Only by understanding what they knew and patterning our faith after theirs can we respond as they did, finding the strength to overcome evil with good, as they did, proving again that all things work together for good for those who are the called according to God's purpose.

The Relationship Must Come First.

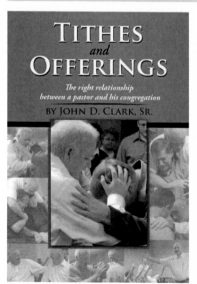

TITHES
and
OFFERINGS

The right relationship between a pastor and his congregation

BY JOHN D. CLARK, SR.

The right relationship between a pastor and his congregation

This is not a book about money. Understanding tithes and offerings is necessary, but the more important issue is the proper relationship of a pastor and his flock, both his responsibility toward them and theirs toward him.

Upon reading this manuscript, one lady commented, "Every sentence will be a new thought to God's people." That may not altogether be the case, but this book certainly will bring new thoughts to those who read it. The lack of understanding about how to deal with God's money has caused much confusion, but be warned; the truth of the matter will challenge your heart. Although the issue of tithes and offerings is a minor matter, as Jesus himself said (Mt. 23:23), if that part of our spiritual life is not in order, every other part of our spiritual life is adversely affected.